The Unsinkable Mary Patten

America's First Female Ship's Captain

By
Thomas T. Wiatt

First published by Limelight Publishing 2022

ISBN (p): 978-1-4710-7794-4
ISBN (e): 978-1-4710-7795-1

Cover design: Thomas T. Wiatt
Layout and typesetting: Limelight Publishing

Limelight Publishing
Po Box 65, Narangba
Brisbane, Queensland Australia 4504

Lulu Press
PO Box 12018
Durham, NC 27709 United States

lulu.com/spotlight/tomwiatt
limelightpublishing.com
lulu.com

Acknowledgments

I would like to personally thank the Mariners' Museum and Park in Newport News, Virginia for the access to their amazing nautical library and for the use of their photo collection.

The painting of Mary Patten used on the front cover was done by Gordon Johnson. This painting was once owned by the Atlantic Marine Insurance Company. Its present location and ownership of the original painting are unknown. Since the Atlantic Marine Insurance Company had an office in the World Trade Center, it is very possible that the original painting was destroyed in the September 11, 2001 attacks of the WTC.

Thanks goes to Elizabeth Lankes for the author's photo.

The painting of the clipper ship, the *Neptune's Car*, on the back cover was done by an unknown Chinese artist in Hong Kong c. 1854.

Vincent DeMasi and get special thanks for his great editing skills.

Thomas T. Wiatt 2022

Introduction

This is the true story of a pregnant teenager who assumed command of an American merchant sailing ship in 1856. She faced off a mutiny, braved gale-force winds and icebergs and then navigated the ship safely to port. Her name was Mary Patten.

Mary Ann Patten was the first woman to pilot a commercial sailing ship. Only a few women could rival this claim. One would be the river pirate Sadie Farrell (aka. Sadie the Goat) who would have been a decade earlier, however, there exists doubt as to her historical existence.

There was also Rachel Wall, Anne Bonny, Mary Reed and Ingela Gathenhielm who were pirates alongside their pirate husbands or partners, but there is little evidence that they actually commanded or navigated a ship.

Eleanor Prentiss Creesy was the only child of a sea captain who taught his daughter sailing and navigational skills. Eleanor married Captain Josiah Cressy in 1841and when Captain Cressy became the commander of the clipper the *Flying Cloud* in 1851, Eleanor helped with the navigation. She never, however, was in command of the vessel.

Harriet Tubman helped lead a boat-based raid on plantations in 1859, but that was three years after Mary's voyage.

Another captain's wife, named Hannah Rebecca Crowell claimed to have commanded a ship, but her story was strangely similar to that of Mary Patten's, and it would have been a month after Mary ended her voyage. Crowell wrote about her sailing experience years later and many historians believe it to be fiction since there was no historical data to back it up.

Zheng Yi Sao (also known as Ching Shih,) who, after the death of her husband in 1807, took control of his Chinese pirate confederation of 400 ships and 60,000 or more pirates. She did command many ships and was one of history's most successful pirates. History, however, does not tell us if she participated in the actual navigation of a ship as did Mary Patten, but she probably comes closest to being the first female ship commander.

Today, women are in command of aircraft carriers; still, Mary Ann Brown Patten's story is unique, and she certainly has the honor of being the first woman to command and navigate a merchant sailing vessel.

-Thomas T. Wiatt 2022

Some are born great, some achieve greatness,
and some have greatness thrust upon them

-William Shakespeare

Contents

Mary Ann Brown Patten 1857
National Portrait Gallery

Chapter 1
The Maiden Voyage

Never, in these United States, has the brain of man conceived, or the hand of man fashioned, so perfect a thing as a clipper ship.

-Samuel Eliot Morison

The *Neptune's Car*[1] was a real beauty. She was a clipper ship built in 1853 at the Gosport Shipyard[2] (the site of today's Norfolk Naval Shipyard) in Portsmouth, Virginia. She was modeled after a clipper[3] designed by William Webb (of Webb Institute[4] fame.) The *Neptune's Car* was built for speed with her ends very sharp, and with slightly concave lines. She weighed 1600 tons (1400 metric tons,) was 216 feet (66 m) stem to stern, with a beam of 40 feet (12 m) and over 23 feet (7 m) tall. The tallest of her three masts stretched 20 feet (6 m) above the deck, and she carried 25 sails, the largest of which spread some 70 feet (21 m) across. Her keel and frame were made from live oak, her hull fashioned from cedar. Unusual for the times, a private bathroom was installed in the captain's quarters. The ship even sported a figurehead[5] of King Neptune[6] wielding his trident under the prow.[7]

After the *Neptune's Car* was launched into Virginia's Elizabeth River on April 16, 1853, she was put into dry dock so that the coppering[8] and rigging of the vessel could be completed. The *Neptune's Car* was then towed on May 8, 1853 to New York's East River, arriving two days later.

She was nearly ready to take her first run to San Francisco, California with a cargo of much needed miner's equipment during California's gold rush. The *Neptune's Car's* journey was delayed until October due to problems with the loading of cargo and finding a suitable captain. The ship's owners finally decided on a man from New Haven, Connecticut, named Samuel Forbes.

After the captain had been hired, they needed a crew. Hiring crew for the *Neptune's Car* was difficult. This was not just because being a seaman on a clipper ship was very hard work. The duties of a crew member of a fast clipper ship included scrubbing bird poop off the oak decks, hoisting rain-drenched sails, and climbing up into the masts as icy waves sometimes swept over the sides of the ship. These were not the reasons. The main reason it was difficult to hire a crew was that Captain Samuel Forbes was not too well liked in the sailing community around New York because of his violent reputation. He a was small man, quick tempered and quick with his fists.

When a crew was finally hired, the *Neptune's Car* was ready for its maiden voyage on October 15. It was arranged for the tugboat, the *Huntress,* to tow the *Neptune's Car* down New York's East River and then out into New York Bay, where the clipper anchored awaiting favorable winds before crossing the bar[9] at Sandy Hook.[10] Captain Forbes ordered all sails set, and the *Neptune's Car* was soon traveling at 14 knots[11]into the Atlantic.

During this voyage, 23 crew members mutinied citing beatings and being worked too hard as the reasons. The crew was even lied to about the destination of the voyage. They thought that they were going just to San Francisco and returning to New York. They did not know that they were also making the long voyage across the Pacific to India.

The ship's commander, Samuel Forbes, had all 23 mutineers confined below deck without food or water as the remaining crew of 7 were force to man the ship. Commander Forbes was able to replenish his crew with more members from a steamer called the *Dwarkanauth* at port in Bengali, India.

Commander Forbes told the captain of a passing ship loudly enough for all to hear:

> I intend to use my authority on the high seas. My revolvers are loaded, and I intend to use them if necessary. Even though the crew all swear they will not go to sea, nor do any work. They'll either work or face being shot.

Many of the mutineers were allowed to return to their duties when they agreed to a reduction in pay and to turn in all weapons[12] in their possession.

Upon returning to New York City, some of the mutineers were arrested, but with the help of some New York lawyers, they charged Captain Forbes with brutality and unlawful beatings. The consequence of this action was that Forbes was relieved of command of the *Neptune's Car*. The ship would need a new captain for a scheduled 1855 around the world voyage.

Gosport Shipyard (Today's Norfolk Naval Shipyard) c.1833
U.S. Navy Archives

King Neptune Figurehead
Mariners' Museum and Park

A typical Clipper Ship from the 1850s
Mariners' Museum and Park

Chapter 2
A New Commander

There can be only one Captain to a ship.

-Thomas John Barnardo

There were many applications to fill the vacancy for the captain position on the *Neptune's Car*. Because of the past mutiny, the ship's owners, Foster & Nickerson Company, wanted a more compassionate man to be the *Neptune's Car's* commander. They decided to take a chance on a young, 26-year-old man named Joshua Patten. Patten was given only a twelve days' notice before he was to ship out.

There are no known images of Joshua Patten, but he was described to have been a handsome young man, tall, and with light brown hair. Patten was well-liked and respected by those who knew him.

Although considered very young for the task of commanding a clipper ship the size of the *Neptune's Car*, Patten had some experience commanding the ship the *Flying Scud*[13] on voyages from New York to Liverpool, England, without incident. The only issue with Patten was that he insisted on bringing his 17-year-old wife, Mary, on the voyage, not wanting to leave her at home alone.

The ship's owners were okay with Mary tagging along but were concerned about how the crew would react to a woman on board. It was commonly believed, among this superstitious lot of sailors, that a woman on board would bring bad luck and incite violent seas. This superstition plus the crew's belief that the ship was cursed because of the former munity, only added to their anxiety.

Captain Joshua Patten's wife Mary, was charismatic, well-spoken, highly educated from fine Boston schools,[14] and every bit her husband's intellectual equal. It was said that she had exceled in mathematics in school. This petite, young lady with long brown hair and dark eyes was born Mary Ann Brown in Chelsea, Massachusetts, in 1837. She was the oldest of George and Elizabeth Brown's children having three younger brothers and one younger sister.[15] Mary was from a nautical family; her English immigrant father having owned a shipbuilding company in nearby Boston. Mary probably met Joshua through some mutual maritime connections in the port of Boston, perhaps at a ship launching ceremony at her father's shipyard.

Mary Ann Brown married sea captain Joshua Adams Patten in 1853 at Boston's Old North Church. This was the very same church whose steeple hoisted two lanterns signaling that the British were advancing toward Concord and Lexington by sea at the start of the American Revolutionary War. Mary was just a few days short of her 16th birthday on her wedding day. Joshua was 25. The couple settled in Boston.

At the time of their wedding. Joshua was employed ferrying cargo and passengers from New York to Boston. Joshua (or Josh, as Mary called him) was originally from Rockland, Maine. He was the oldest of six children of Sarah M. Patten.[16] Some of Joshua's brothers were also sailors.

Joshua Patten's first voyage as captain of the *Neptune's Car* was an ambitious one because he would be sailing seas that neither he nor his ship had any experience with and for a much longer time than usual. On this 1855 voyage the *Neptune's Car* was to encircle the globe using only wind (no steam power was available on this ship) and do it quickly, but Captain Patten felt confident that he was up to the task.

Captain Patten's mission was to sail south from New York City and then through the treacherous seas around South America's Cape Horn.[17] The next stop would be San Francisco where their cargo would be unloaded. In addition, this voyage required the *Neptune's Car* to sail all the way across the Pacific to Hong Kong, China, to buy tea. From Hong Kong, they would continue westward past India, around South Africa's southern cape, and then north to Deal, England, to unload the tea bought in the Orient. Afterwards the *Neptune's Car* would return to its home port in New York City with goods bought in England. With a few exceptions, this voyage would go pretty much as planned.

The *Flying Scud* c.1859
Painting by William G. Vorke
Mariners' Museum and Park

New York 1850s
The Bowery Boys

Chapter 3
Mary's Maiden Voyage

The sea that calls all things unto her calls me, and I must embark.

-Kahlil Gibran

Mr. and Mrs. Patten moved into the captain's cabin the first week of January 1855 and got ready for their first voyage together. They got settled in, as Mary tried to make their cabin feel like home. The captain's cabin now had a certain woman's touch, unusual for a captain's quarters. In the meantime, Captain Patten carefully studied the charts and directions set down in the recently published guidebooks by Matthew Fontaine Maury.[18]

A few days later, on January 13, 1855, the *Neptune's Car* was ready to sail out of New York harbor. A steam powered tugboat[19] towed the ship out into the narrows and into Sandy Hook. Once abreast of the Sandy Hook lighthouse,[20] the tug's tow line was released, and the *Neptune's Car* was off on her voyage. The winds were from the northwest. They sailed south towards Bermuda, hoping to catch some trade winds.

As exciting as this world cruise might sound, there would be few stops. By the time they had crossed the Equator near the coast of Brazil, Mary became bored. She passed the time by reading all the limited medical books on board and became the self-appointed, but much needed, nurse for the crew. Mary also helped with some of the cooking on board.

Mary also became curious about how to operate the ship's sextant[21] and wanted her husband to teach her how to find the ship's position on the charts. She proved to have a rare talent for the mathematical calculations required to accurately determine the ship's position. Mary greatly impressed her proud husband with the fact that her calculations were even more accurate than his.

Captain Patten told his wife that, if given the opportunity, she would make an excellent ship's captain. She believed it. By the time the *Neptune's Car* reached San Francisco, Mary was a proficient navigator, and she was beginning to earn the respect of the crew because of her nursing skills.

Seeing San Francisco must have been exciting for Mary, who had rarely left her home of Boston in her entire life. There was little time to sightsee, however, for the vessel was quickly unloaded and then refilled with sand and rocks for ballast for the next stop, Hong Kong.

The *Neptune's Car* left San Francisco on May 13, 1855. Violent tropical storms brought the only relief from the heat as the *Neptune's Car* slowly sailed toward the Orient. Mary, now 18, refined her navigational skills with the habit of making regular daily star sightings allowing her to gain an accurate fix on their exact position. They finally arrived in Hong Kong's Victoria Harbor on July 2, 1855, joining dozens of other ships from nations all over the world.

The Chinese tea they hoped to load aboard was not yet available in Hong Kong, so Captain and Mrs. Patten had a great deal of time to wander the many shops, markets, and bazaars on the Hong Kong waterfront. One can only imagine what souvenirs and gifts they might have purchased and what sights they may have seen.

Captain Patten was soon notified that tea would be available in the Chinese port of Foochow, a short sail northeast up the Chinese coast. This leg of their journey would not be without potential danger, because Britain and China were engaged in the Second Opium War,[22] plus pirates often roamed this region. The *Neptune's Car* was well armed with small iron cannons and swivel guns, but, fortunately, they never needed to be fired on this peaceful voyage.

An incident happened in Hong Kong shortly before the *Neptune's Car's* departure that demonstrated Mary's influence upon her husband. The only Americans in Hong Kong were a few Christian missionaries. One of these Hong Kong missionaries, named Otis Gibson, was appointed missionary to Foochow but he had no way to get there. Finding out that the *Neptune's Car* was headed for Foochow, Gibson went to see Captain Patten to ask if he could "hitch a ride." When Gibson arrived at the ship, he learned that the captain was at shore, and he was directed to approach Mrs. Patten about this matter.

Otis Gibson told Mary Patten of his dilemma. She politely told Gibson that they could not take any passengers and that there was just no room for him. Gibson said that his wife would be very disappointed to hear that. Mary quickly responded:

> Oh, is there a Mrs. Gibson? I have not seen a white woman for over five months. Why yes, Josh can take you as well as not, I'll have a stateroom cleared out right away.[23]

The *Neptune's Car* departed for Foochow to acquire tea on August 1, 1855, and the crew and passengers had a very pleasant trip to Foochow arriving on August 12, 1855. Mary said goodbye to Mr. and Mrs. Gibson as they disembarked. Mrs. Gibson said that the voyage was "delightful." It is certain that Mary enjoyed some female company, even if it was just for a little while.

It was not until September 28 that the ship was fully loaded with its cargo of Chinese tea. The next morning a tug towed the *Neptune's Car* out to sea. Captain Patten was fully aware of the dangerous hidden rocks and shoals that could quickly sink a ship if a captain was not careful.

Captain Patten set sail to the south, but the ship was hit by a vicious monsoon with winds coming from the southwest. The *Neptune's Car* was forced into the Taiwan Strait and had to anchor in Taiwan for the time being. Mary Patten was helping a great deal with her navigational skills at this point.

Leaving Taiwan when it was safe, the ship sailed south towards Borneo, Indonesia, through the treacherous pirate territory of the Gaspar Strait, then through the Malacca Strait without incident. Despite the fact that Captain Patten had never sailed these seas before, he was confident in the crew's abilities, the ship's seaworthiness, and most of all, his wife's navigational skills.

Finally, the *Neptune's Car* raced across the Indian Ocean and rounded the southern cape of Africa, where they were able to hit the Agulhas Current,[24] then north to England. The ship arrived and was guided into the berth in Deal, England, on January 19, 1856. There, they unloaded the tea that was purchased in the Orient. The *Neptune's Car* did not depart England until February 27, 1856, long enough for the crew and the Pattens to spend some time there.

From England, home must have seemed nearby as it was only just across the Atlantic. When just barely out of British waters King Neptune's evil curse made its presence known. The wind direction suddenly shifted northwest to southwest several times, causing the ship to tack[25] numerous times. The crew was ordered to shorten the sails. In the process, a sailor named John Kearn lost his grip on the mainsail yard and fell to his death. Mary rushed to his aid, but there was nothing that she could do. Kearn had been with the original crew of the *Neptune's Car* during the maiden voyage. He was buried at sea the next day.

Their bad luck continued when they were only a few nautical miles from the port of New York City. On the morning of March 23, 1856, during a vicious thunderstorm, lightning struck the forward mast. The wood splinted, and many of the crew who were working the sails fell to the deck, and some were badly burned. Mary was quick to help these men and nursed their wounds for the remainder of the voyage. She was beginning to win the love and respect of the crew. Many crew members who had an aversion to a woman being aboard a ship were beginning to change their minds.

Within 20 nautical miles from New Jersey's Sandy Hook lighthouse, the winds completely died down and the ship barely moved for three days. Finally, on March 29, the wind did pick up, and the lighthouse at Sandy Hook was sighted. Captain Patten hoisted his ensign[26] atop the foremast, and the tugboat, the *Huntress,* appeared and towed the *Neptune's Car* safely into New York harbor, and she was tied up at Pier 9 in Lower Manhattan.

San Francisco 1850s
Oakland Museum of California

Hong Kong, Victoria Harbor c. 1860

Sandy Hook Inlet and Lighthouse
Painting by Edward Moran

Chapter 4
The Second Voyage's Preparations

If a ship is strong, the ocean's tides do not bother it.

-Matshona Dhliwayo

It would be a couple of months until the *Neptune's Car* was ready for the next voyage scheduled for July 1856. The forward mast needed to be replaced, and much of the rigging needed to be repaired. The *Neptune's Car* also needed re-caulking, re-coppering, and some sail repairs were badly needed. Again, Joshua Patten would be the captain, and he came to New York City from Boston to supervise the ship's repairs.

Through some negotiations with the ship's owners (Foster & Nickerson,) Captain Patten was able to get a pay raise for himself and the crew. As before, Mary would accompany her husband on this voyage, but, of course, she would not be paid. She was now 19 years old and pregnant, although she may not have known of her condition at the time.

This time it would be a much shorter, 15,000 nautical mile[27] trip. They would sail from New York City to San Francisco. The ship would have a cargo of machinery for gold mines, as well as iron and other much needed supplies that would be worth about $13 million in today's money.

Captain Patten could expect to earn $3,000 (about $350,000 in today's money) for a successful voyage, but if he could complete it in less than 100 days, he would be entitled to as much as $5,000 (about $583,000 in today's money.) Captain Patten's previous voyage from New York to San Francisco took 100 days and 23 hours. That was considered a very good time, but he hoped to shorten it considerably on this voyage. This would require expert navigation, favorable winds, and a devoted and skilled crew.

The crew probably had all but forgotten about the ship being cursed because of a woman being on board, when the first mate had severely fractured his leg while overseeing the loading of the ship's cargo. The *Neptune's Car*'s owners refused to delay the voyage and were certainly not going to wait for the first mate's leg to heal. They had to find a suitable replacement. Their valuable cargo of supplies for the California gold-mining camps could not wait, and they were guaranteed high profits if the ship arrived in San Francisco quickly.

Without Captain Patten's knowledge or consent, the ship's owners hired a man from Philadelphia named William Keeler. Keeler was unknown in New York and had questionable credentials, but the ship's owners were anxious that the *Neptune's Car* would leave on time. It would be soon discovered that the curse, if there was one, did not result in the first mate fracturing his leg, but in the hiring of William Keeler. He would turn out to be a problem.

The second and third mates were William Hare and George Kingsley, respectively. Both were on previous *Neptune's Car* voyages and were a bit "rough around the edges" and illiterate. They were considered to be brutes by the rest of the crew, however, were said to be good at obeying the captain's orders. Keeler and third mate Kingsley became friends during the voyage and were sometimes "partners in crime."

The *Neptune's Car* and crew set sail on July 1, 1856, as a tug towed her out to sea. The New York waterfront temperatures were in the upper 90s F (30s C) as sailors hoped for cooler temperatures in the open water away from shore. Captain Patten mentioned to Mary that he was not feeling well and was having headaches and was fatigued. Mary attributed this to the stress that he may had acquired on his first voyage with the *Neptune's Car*. She would be wrong.

A Wooden Clipper Ship in New York City Dry Dock
New York City Archives

Chapter 5
Keeler

The sea does not reward those who are too anxious, too greedy, or too impatient.

-Anne Morrow Lindbergh

The *Neptune's Car* and four other similar clipper ships, the *Romance of the Seas,* the *Intrepid,* the *Rapid,* and the *Bald Eagle,* all left New York for San Francisco at about the same time. It was common practice in those days for gamblers to make bets with New York bookies about which ship would arrive in San Francisco first. Captain Patten, himself, even bet that the *Neptune's Car* would win the race. One of many problems with hiring Keeler as first mate is that he had placed a bet that the *Neptune's Car* would *lose*. Keeler would do everything that he could think of on board to make sure the ship's voyage would be a failure.

Even though Captain Patten and first mate Keeler were responsible for tracking the ships position and course, the captain was relying on Mary to review and confirm their findings.

Captain Patten was quick to have misgivings about first mate Keeler. On several occasions the second mate, William Hare, found Keeler asleep in the chart house when he was supposed to be on watch. This could be very dangerous for a ship for the lookout to be asleep. Hare most likely reported Keeler's insubordination to Captain Patten.

Captain Patten himself caught Keeler asleep when he came on deck to check the ship's course, wind, and speed. First, the captain noticed that a sail had been taken down in spite of his direct orders given to Keeler to the contrary. The captain went looking for Keeler to complain and found him asleep. The captain was understandably angry, and the two men began a shouting match that almost came to blows. Captain Patten told first mate Keeler that, if his disobedience continued, he would be relieved of his first mate duties.

Just off the coast of Brazil, Captain Patten gave orders to Keeler that the sails be set, but the first mate refused to obey. To make matters worse, Keeler was defiant in front of the crew. Joshua Patten's headaches were getting worse, and he was beginning to feel ill, and the stress he was getting from Keeler was not helping.

Because of his illness, Captain Patten was relying on Mary's navigational skills more and more. It was no longer a secret from the crew that Mary was helping with the navigation of the ship. On many occasions, she was spotted on deck with the sextant determining the ship's position. Keeler was probably upset and resentful that the captain's wife was confirming his own nautical measurements.

By the time the *Neptune's Car* passed the eastern tip of Brazil at a place called Cabo Soa Roque, Captain Patten had lost his patience with William Keeler. With the use of his pistol, Captain Patten arrested Keeler, had the crew members place him in irons, and confined him to his cabin. Mary and the crew must have been shocked by the uncharacteristic anger in the captain's voice.

Captain Patten now had to perform the duties of both captain and first mate. These duties were even more exhausting considering the captain's ill health. While approaching the Falkland Islands, the *Neptune's Car* was being hammered with snow and sleet and violent rains. The weather was so bad that Captain Patten considered retreating to the port of Rio de Janeiro, Brazil, or Buenos Aires, Argentina for safety. Perhaps, he must have thought that he could hire a new first mate and get some much-needed repairs done to the *Neptune's Car* at one of those ports. Captain Patten decided, for better or for worse, to press on.

A Clipper Ship in a Hurricane
Mariners' Museum and Park

Model of an 1853 Clipper Ship similar to that of the
Neptune's Car
Mariners' Museum and Park

Chapter 6
Joshua's Illness

Through sickness and in health.

-Mathew 28:20 KJV

To ensure that the ship remained on course, Captain Patten did not leave the ship's deck for eight days and nights through all types of weather. Exhausted from lack of sleep, he began to feel even more ill, but continued to perform his duties. As the ship began to approach the most dangerous part of its journey, the captain collapsed on deck.

Some of the crewmen found Captain Patten and carried him below to his bunk. He struggled violently, out of his head with fever, as they struggled to lay him down. He was soon very ill with fever, pneumonia, and tuberculosis meningitis[28] (an illness that was prevalent in the 1800s.) Mary had the crew tie the captain to his bed to keep him from being thrown off as the ship rolled in the heavy waves.

As Captain Patten's condition worsened, Mary searched through the ship's medical books, hoping to find the cause and treatment for his symptoms. Captain Patten soon was afflicted with periods of blindness and deafness. Mary shaved his head and sponged his forehead with cool water to try to reduce his fever, but there was little that she could do.

Soon, Captain Patten's condition got worse as the infection spread to his optic nerves. Sometimes he would become comatose or have feverish hallucinations. Patten's periods of blindness and deafness continued.

To make matters worse, the *Neptune's Car* was caught in a horrendous gale. Waves threatened to engulf the ship. With the first mate, Keller, in irons, the second mate, William Hare, took the helm. He knew how to handle the ship but had no idea how to navigate. They were approaching the unpredictable winds and currents around Cape Horn and their situation was desperate. Everyone in the crew must have been asking themselves, "Who will navigate the ship?"

William Hare requested to Mary that she navigate the ship. With no other options she agreed. Mary now needed to convince the crew that she was competent in the skills of navigation and that the second mate, Hare, could handle the ship. She assembled the crew upon the quarterdeck[29] and explained the situation.

There are no exact records of what was said, but Mary explained to the crew the condition of her husband and that she would navigate if they would allow it. She appealed to the crew to stand by and have faith in her.

The crew may have been shocked or confused at first, having no idea that they were about to make history. After some talk among themselves, the crew unanimously agreed to obey this 19-year-old woman's commands. Mary Ann Patten suddenly became the first woman to officially command a merchant vessel.

Sextant c. 1850
Mariners' Museum and Park

Chapter 7
Mary, Mary, Quite Contrary

Courage is not the absence of fear, but the conquest of it.

-William Danforth

Hearing of Captain Patten's illness, and that Mary was now in command, former first mate Keller protested from his quarters and demanded that he be released and given command of the ship. Keller even sent Mary a letter, urging her to turn the ship around and head back to New York. He even threatened to start a mutiny. His demands were ignored by Mary and the crew. Mary told Keller that her husband did not trust him and neither did she. Keller still tried, without success, to get the crew to mutiny against Mary Patten.

With her skills, Mary Patten guided the *Neptune's Car* safely through the Strait of Le Maire, between the southern tip of Argentina and States Island,[30] in spite of the tricky tides and currents. Then, the trouble started. The *Neptune's Car* needed to sail west in order to get around the cape, but strong, westerly, 100-mph (160 kph) storm winds and 50-foot (15 m) waves slamming against the ship made it impossible. There was a real fear that the ship might crash into the 600 ft (183 m) high cliffs of Cape Horn's jagged coastline.

Mary Patten's next decision was one that only an experienced ship's commander would have made. She directed the (now new first mate) William Hare to sail east and then south in order to sail around the storm. This decision worked for avoiding the storm, but it brought them dangerously close to icebergs in the freezing waters of the Drake Passage[31]near Antarctica.

Mary ordered the *Neptune's Car* westward again, and the men climbed the rigging to set the sails. Soon after a 15-

year-old lookout in the crow's nest[32] noticed a haze surrounding the clouds off the ship's port side. Crewmen who had experienced previous voyages around Cape Horn knew that the haze meant icebergs ahead. On Mary's order, the men scrambled back up the rigging to take in the sails and to slow the ship's progress, knowing that one wrong move and the *Neptune's Car* could strike an iceberg, above or below the water surface and be lost.

Mary doubled the number of crew members to watch for icebergs. The still air was so freezing that there was a real danger of crew members getting hypothermia. To prevent this, Mary changed lookouts every 30 minutes. For four days, Mary Patten and William Hare alternated watches upon the deck as they guided the clipper through massive ice mountains. When Mary was not on deck, she was below nursing her husband. His high fever was her primary concern.

Mary, with 18 days of command experience, managed to navigate around the icebergs with no casualties. As the *Neptune's Car* made it around Cape Horn, it then sailed north up the coast of Chile to warmer climes. As the weather improved, so did Joshua's condition. He was able to hear and speak somewhat and was becoming more coherent.

Even though Captain Patten did not quite have full use of his faculties, he was made aware of the situation. Mary told her husband that she was navigating the ship and that she and William Hare had been taking turns being on watch through the iceberg infested waters of Antarctica.

Captain Patten personally thanked his wife and temporary first mate Hare for their service. He felt that they deserved a break from all their work and then made a very bad decision. Much to Mary's horror, Patten decided to restore William Keeler to his position as first officer on a probationary basis. This change in heart may have been because the captain feared the crew might mutiny and even physically attack his wife. The thought of Mary being raped was never far from his mind. He may have felt that putting Keeler back in charge might appease any mutiny-minded crew members. William Keeler would now be the navigator.

One of the first things Keeler did was to take possession of the ship's sextant and compass so that only he (and not Mary) could navigate. Keeler forbade Mary from taking part in any of the navigational tasks.

By observing the position of the sun, Mary felt that Keeler was navigating east toward the coast of Chile and not north to San Francisco. Mary told her husband about her misgiving about Keeler, and Captain Patten became suspicious, too. The captain and Mary built a compass by magnetizing a sewing needle that floated on a small piece of wood in a glass of water. This was all done without Keller's knowledge.

At the voyage's beginning, the ship's owners gave Captain Patten strict instructions that the *Neptune's Car* was not to be taken to any foreign port, except in an emergency. There was a fear that, in a foreign port, the $350,000 ($13 million in today's money) cargo would be stolen by thieves, pirates, or even government officials who may not have been too friendly to the United States. Neither Captain Patten nor Mary was prepared to sacrifice the cargo entrusted to them.

Taking the ship to a foreign port was exactly what Keeler was trying to do. He was intentionally headed for the city of Valparaiso, Chile. Maybe he knew that Captain Patten would have him arrested if and when the ship anchored at an American port, and he planned to "jump" ship.

Keller's motives were confirmed to Mary by Captain Patten's makeshift compass. Upon learning this, Captain Patten had Keeler arrested, put in irons, and confined again, this time for good. Patten then gave orders that under no circumstances, was the *Neptune's Car* to be taken into any other port than San Francisco.

Days later, Captain Patten fell back into a deep coma. Mary was the commander once again.

Cape Horn, Chile

A Crow's Nest
British Library

Chapter 8
Onward to San Francisco

...San Francisco is a lady.

-Norman Mailer

As commander, Mary tried to make up for lost time due to Keeler's Chilean side trip. The trade winds blew strong and steady, and Mary kept every available sail aloft. These favorable winds did not last, however, and the ship hardly moved for 10 days. The tropical heat at the equator made Captain Patten's condition worse and was having an effect on Mary as well. She was now 6 months pregnant and suffering from exhaustion. The winds did finally pick up and on November 11, 1856, they were soon to be in sight of San Francisco.

William Hare fired a rocket to announce the ship's arrival as the ensign was raised to the foretop.[33] A tugboat was sent out to guide the *Neptune's Car* through the Boca del Puerto de San Francisco (now called the Golden Gate Strait) on November 15, 1856. Mary was at the helm and navigated the ship into the port. The *Neptune's Car* was tied up at the Folsom Street Wharf.

After 25 days of Mary being in command of the *Neptune's Car,* the vessel reached San Francisco. It had been 120 days since they left New York City on this history-making voyage. This was not the 100 days that Captain Patten had hope for, but, under the circumstances, it was a very speedy time. The safety of the ship, the arrival of the cargo and the preservation of her husband's life were completely due to the constant care and watchfulness of Mrs. Mary Ann Patten.

As for the race to San Francisco between the clipper ships, The *Neptune's Car* came in 2nd place out of the four ships that left New York on that fateful day of July 1, 1856. The clipper ship the *Romance of the Sea* had arrived a few days before.

William Keeler knew that he would be arrested as soon as the ship docked at San Francisco. Even before the ship had reached her final destination, Keeler, with the help of the third mate, George Kingsley, was able to get unchained and jumped ship while the ship was still in midstream. William Keeler was never heard from again.[34]

Soon after the *Neptune's Car* was towed onto San Francisco's Folsom Street Wharf. The vessel's second mate, William Hare, shouted a demand for help in lifting Captain Patten onto a makeshift stretcher. Hare received help from plenty of volunteers. The crew truly loved their captain and Mrs. Patten, as well. Astonishingly, she later revealed that her busy schedule throughout the voyage didn't permit her the time to change out of her clothes for 50 days.

The proud captain appeared thin and frail, and his face was ghostly gray. Dockworkers were even more curious by the appearance of a young woman amongst the all-male crew. From the roundness of her midsection, she was noticeably pregnant, but she stayed near her husband, Joshua, as he was carried to a local San Francisco hospital. Arrangements were made for a nearby hotel room for Mary by the New York insurance company that insured the ship and its contents.

Forever grateful that she safely delivered the ship and cargo, the insurance company (Atlantic Mutual Insurance Company) gave Mary a reward check for $1,000 (approximately $115,000 in today's money) and a note of thanks. She, however, received no other payment from the ship's owners for her captain or nursing duties, nor did Captain Patten for the time he was unable to perform his duties. But Mary was, however, grateful and humble in her appreciation of the insurance company's support. She wrote them a thank you note:

> I received yesterday your communication of the 18th …
> and it is with mingled sensations of gratitude and embarrassment that I leave my post as a watcher by my husband's sick bed to reply. I am sincerely grateful to you and to all those you represent for the very kind expression of sympathy, and for the liberal enclosure which you have transmitted to me on their behalf…
>
> Be assured, gentlemen, that through all the truth which may be before me, and while I live, your considerate kindness will ever be held in thankful remembrance by yours,
>
> very respectfully.
>
> Mary A. Patten

Mary Patten stunned the maritime world by safely rounding Cape Horn and delivering her cargo to San Francisco on time and intact. If social media had existed in 1856, the news of Mary Patten's accomplishments would have gone viral. The news did, however, go global. Newspapers around the world picked up this story. Eager reporters from far away began piecing together the sad but inspiring tale. The New York Daily Times gave Mary credit for keeping her husband alive during the voyage. When word spread of how she had nursed her husband, navigated the ship, and protected the vessel's cargo, all at the age of 19 and pregnant she became an instant celebrity.

Most of the information came from the crew and certainly not from Mary herself. She was far too humble to give any interviews and was too busy nursing her husband to even consider it.

The newspapers wrote articles entitled: *Heroic Conduct of a Woman, A Heroine Arrived, The Florence Nightingale of the Sea* and *Heroine of the Sea.* One paper referred to her as a "Quick-Learning Wife," another called her "Young, Tough, and Pregnant." *The New York Times* even called her "A Wife Worth Having," as if most wives were not. None of these labels were wanted nor sought after by Mary Patten.

Broadway Wharf, San Francisco c. 1850s
Oakland Museum of California Collection

Broadway Wharf, San Francisco c. 1860
Society of California Pioneers Photography Collection

Chapter 9
Return to Boston

Every traveler returns home.

-David Levithan

The *Neptune's Car*'s owners hired another captain to sail the ship back to New York. As Joshua struggled for his life in a local hospital, the Pattens were left to find their own way back to Boston.

Joshua was a Free Mason,[35] and he received assistance from the California Masonic Temple that also sent fellow Mason, Dr. Harris, to accompany the Pattens back to Boston and to provide medical care.

In January 1857, Mr. and Mrs. Patten finally began their strenuous, two-month return to Boston. The first leg of the journey was to Panama by steamboat.

The Pattens and company arrived in Panama City, then they traveled by the newly constructed rail[36] through the jungles of Panama until they arrived at the brand-new port city of Aspinwall, Panama.[37]

From the Aspinwall, they boarded the steamship the *George Law* to New York. In New York the couple were taken to the Battery Hotel where Joshua and Mary were placed under the care of local doctors. Captain Patten's condition worsened significantly on the steamships and railroads that transported him home. Patten's medical care and needs were paid for by the ship's owners.

Mary and Joshua returned to Boston on February 19, 1857. They were accompanied by friends plus Mary's brother who oversaw their needs. A local Boston society of ladies managed to raise $1400 (about $163,000 in today's money) to help the Pattens with their expenses. Occasionally, Joshua would speak to Mary, but not lucidly, rather in a wild and incoherent manner.

Mary gave birth to a son named Joshua Adams Patten, Jr. on March 10, 1857, less than 3 weeks after Mary and Joshua had arrived in Boston. Joshua's condition by this point, was so bad and he was so incoherent that he did not even know that he had a son.

Captain Joshua Patten would never recover. He died of tuberculosis on July 25, 1857, at the age of 30. The city of Boston observed a period of mourning by flying harbor flags at half-mast and ringing church bells. The *Boston Courier* newspaper set up a fund, giving Mary $1399 (about $163,000 in today's money) to help defray the costs of caring for her husband. Mary wrote this poetic inscription and had it carved in stone and placed at his grave site:

> Are there seas in heaven, Joshua?
> And is there such a vessel as our
> Neptune's Car? If there is, wait for
> me, and we shall explore the vast
> and boundless reaches of eternity

For the next four years, Mary lived in Boston's North End with her mother and son. Perhaps the Neptune's curse haunted her, for on March 15, 1861, Mary Ann Brown Patten also died of tuberculosis, most likely caught from her husband. She died just short of her 24th birthday.

Her son Joshua, Jr., was then raised by his grandmother, Elizabeth Brown, after the death of his mother Mary. He grew up to be a carriage painter. Joshua, Jr. never married and tragically died in an accidental drowning in Rockland, Maine, in 1900, at age 43. Mary, Joshua and Joshua, Jr, are all buried together at the Woodlawn Cemetery in Everett, Massachusetts.

At the U.S. Merchant Marine Academy in King's Point, New York, all the buildings are named after famous nautical men, except one. The hospital on the campus is named "The Patten Hospital," in honor of the first female merchant vessel commander.

Panama Railroad c. 1855
Panama Railroad Archives

Boston Harbor c. 1850

Chapter 10
Neptune's Curse

Tell her this and more, —
That the king of the seas, weeps too

-Stephen Crane

Unfortunately, the *Neptune's Car* was built near the tail end of the great clipper ship era. Steamships were becoming more and more popular and the opening of the Suez Canal in 1858 made around the world voyages much quicker by bypassing Africa. The need for fast, but sometimes unreliable, clipper ships was no longer needed.

The American Civil War also proved a disaster to the American clipper ship era. Dozens of the finest vessels were captured and destroyed by Confederate raiders. At the beginning of the Civil War, it was discovered that one of the *Neptune's Car's* co-owners was a Confederate named James Wright. This was even more ironic considering that the *Neptune's Car* had been bringing supplies to northern forts. Upon learning of the ship's Confederate co-owner, the Federal Government impounded the ship. The U.S. government released the ship after James Wright's portion of shares in the vessel had been bought out by the other stockholders.

In February 1863, the *Neptune's Car* was sold at auction in Liverpool, England to a British shipping company. It may have been difficult finding a buyer because many sailors believed the *Neptune's Car* was a cursed ship.

The sailors may have had good reason for this superstition. A series of hardships, mutinies, mishaps, and tragedies had happened on board this ship in its short lifespan. During its voyages a sailor was murdered, and another was killed in a freak cargo loading accident. A first mate broke his leg. Crew members fell overboard and drowned or fell from a ship's mast and died. On another occasion, a cargo of munitions spilled on board, knocking the crew out with its acidic fumes. Captain Joshua Patten's sudden and unexpected illness also contributed to this superstition.

But she was sold and now sailed under the British flag. There had been some talk among the British buyers about using the *Neptune's Car* as a blockade runner, bringing much needed supplies to the Confederate States, but the ship's owners decided against it thinking it would be too risky.

The final deathblow came to the *Neptune's Car* in 1869 when no tea or cargo charters were awarded to her. In 1870, the ship was sold for her parts, metals, and building materials, and her hull was used for firewood. She had served her purpose.

Perhaps, in some other world, the *Neptune's Car* still exists with Mary Patten at the helm exploring the vast and boundless reaches of eternity with her husband Josh at her side.

Clipper Ship being stripped and burned
Mariners' Museum and Park

Epilogue

Confidence is food for the wise
and liquor for the fool

-Confucius

For whatever reason, Mary was not active in any of the newly organized women's rights movements of that time. Many women's rights organizations still held her accomplishments up as an example of a woman's ability to compete successfully in what was then considered to be a male vocation. Mary resisted any interviews and turned down offers to make speeches, citing that talking about her experiences would only bring back painful memories.

Nonetheless, her accomplishments in her short life were remarkable on many levels. Mary Patten not only had authority over the ship she commanded, but also over the crew of men who sailed it. Getting the absolute loyalty of a male crew would be difficult for a woman even today. Perhaps Mary's position of authority was more acceptable to the ship's crew because she didn't actively seek it out; it was thrusted upon her.

Mary Patten didn't become the first woman to command a U.S. merchant ship because she was the first woman capable of doing so. She was just in the right place at the right time, with the right amount of ability, confidence, and courage.

Mary Patten lived in the Victorian era, when people were modest about their achievements, and she downplayed her own role. The only words Mary Patten, ever wrote about the voyage were to the Atlantic Mutual Insurance Company, where she gave credit to the second mate, William Hare, and the rest of the crew. As for herself, she wrote that her accomplishments were, "…only the plain duty of a wife towards a good husband."

Painting of a Proposed Figure Head of Mary Patten
Shining Sea Foundation

Only 20, she commanded a clipper ship, saved a $10 million cargo

The same marine tradition that shaped Atlantic's insurance protection for *Neptune's Car* produces better insurance for you today

Less than a month out of New York, hull down with cargo for California, the clipper ship *Neptune's Car* encountered multiple misfortune. Captain Joshua Patten had to depose his chief mate for insubordination. Then soon after, he and the two remaining officers fell helplessly ill of malaria.

One person remained able to command: Mary Patten, who as a bride had learned celestial navigation from her husband on her only previous voyage. She assembled the crew and announced her decision. They'd sail on.

For 55 hard-driving days she captained the clipper as it sped down the Atlantic, swept around the Horn, and skimmed up the Pacific. On November 13, 1856, the ship safely entered the Golden Gate. The cargo she delivered would be worth $10,000,000 today.

The Atlantic gave Mrs. Patten a generous reward, for the cargo was covered by an Atlantic policy. Most cargo was in those days. Shippers knew Atlantic stood by its word, paid claims promptly and ungrudgingly. That's the marine insurance way of doing business. This broad-minded approach and spirit of always doing what's best for the policyholder has guided Atlantic for 123 years.

What that means to you today is this: When you insure your car, your home or your business with the Atlantic Companies, you can rely not only on quality insurance protection, but also on fast, fair and ungrudging claim payments for insured losses, in the true tradition of the marine insurer.

And this includes the belief that your interests are best served today when you buy insurance through an independent agent or broker. That's the *only* way Atlantic sells its quality protection.

THE ATLANTIC COMPANIES

ATLANTIC MUTUAL • CENTENNIAL • 45 Wall Street, New York

Ad from The Atlantic Mutual Insurance Company

Author Thomas T. Wiatt

About the Author

Thomas T. Wiatt lives in the port city of Newport News, Virginia not far from where the *Neptune's Car* was constructed. He is a retired engineer from Newport News Shipbuilding and is a third-generation shipbuilder. Tom also volunteers at the Mariners Museum and Park also in Newport News. He is never too far away from the sea.

Thomas T. Wiatt is the author of the books:

Rev. William E. Wiatt, The life and times of a Confederate Chaplain and related family stories.

Captain Sally, A Biography of Capt. Sally Tompkins, America's First Female Army Officer.

Alleged Pirate, The Legend of Captain John Sinclair of Smithfield and Gloucester, Virginia.

Lawyer Walker, A Biography of Thomas Calhoun Walker.

The Stonewall, The true story of a ship without a port.

Gringos, A History of U.S. Citizens in Latin America.

Bibliography

Baker, Julie, *The Troubled Voyage of the Neptune's Car*. American History Journal, 2002.

Clark, Arthur H., *The Clipper Ship Era 1843 – 1869*. 1911.

Clary, James, *Superstitions of the Sea*: A digest of beliefs, customs, and mystery. 1994.

Flanders, Alan, *Clipper Neptune's Car Saved from Disaster by Quick-Learning Wife of Stricken Skipper*. Virginian-Pilot, October 15, 2000.

Furey, Lauren T., *Patten Down the Hatches!* Blog 2020.

Gibson, Eliza, *A Trip to China*. 1916.

Gibson, Eliza, *The Diary of Eliza Gibson*, 1855.

Joy, Arthur F., *Captain's Wife*, 1959.

Kelly, Douglas, *The Captain's Wife*, Penguin Putnam, 2002.

Meroff, Deborah, *Captain, My Captain,* Inheritance Publication,1997.

Nelson, Dawn, *The Unsinkable Mary Patten.* Blog 2021.

New England Historical Society, Mary Patten, 19 and Pregnant, Takes Command of a Clipper Ship in 1856. 2022.

New York Herald. February 18, 1857, *Heroic Conduct of a Woman.*

New York Daily Tribune. February 18, 1857. *A Heroine of the Sea.*

Simpson, Paul W., *Neptune's Car, An American Legend.* 2010.

Vargo, Dina, *Wild Woman of Boston: Mettle and Moxie in the Hub*, 2015.

Webb, Wanda, *Mary of the Neptune's Car*, Yankee, March 1966.

Notes

[1] Before the days of four-wheeled self-mobile vehicles, the word "car" had the archaic meaning for "chariot." In ancient Roman mythology King Neptune rode in a chariot pulled by seahorses.

[2] The Norfolk Naval Shipyard has been building ships since 1767. The site was even used by the British as early as 1852. It was the first shipyard in America to have a dry dock.

[3] A clipper was a type of mid-19th-century merchant sailing vessel designed for speed. Clippers were generally narrow for their length, small by later 19th century standards, could carry limited bulk freight, and had a large total sail area. They were nicknamed "The Greyhounds of the Sea."

[4] Webb Institute is a private engineering college in Glen Cove, New York. Each graduate of Webb Institute earns a degree in naval architecture. Students receive full tuition for four years.

[5] At that time in history, many sailors could not read. This was actually encouraged because it was felt that illiterate sailors were less likely to mutiny. Figureheads on the bow actually provided a function because they helped illiterate sailors identify their ship. In ancient times it was believed that figureheads would warn off evil spirts.

[6] Neptune, sometimes referred to as King Neptune, is the god of the sea in the ancient Roman religion.

[7] A prow is the portion of a ship's bow above water.

[8] Pioneered by the Royal Navy in the 18th century, coppering the hull was an effective way of protecting the wood from the corrosive effects of salt water.

[9] A bar is, in nautical terms, a buildup of sand and silt where an inlet, river, or harbor meets the open ocean.

[10] Sandy Hook is a barrier spit in, New Jersey.

[11] A knot is equal to one nautical mile per hour.

[12] The crew had many weapons because of a fear of pirate attacks.

[13] The Flying Scud was a clipper ship launched at the Metcalf & Norris Shipyard in Damarico, Maine in 1853.

[14] In **1789** Massachusetts was the first state in the nation to pass a comprehensive education law.

---

[15] 1850 U.S. Census Boston, Ward 2, Massachusetts

[16] 1850 U.S. Census Rockland, Maine., The census does not mention Joshua's father and it assumed that he was dead at this time.

[17] Officially called "Cabo de Hornos."

[18] Matthew Fontaine Maury (1806 – 1873) was an American naval officer who mapped the oceans' currents earning him the nickname the "Pathfinder of the Seas." He published *Physical Geography of the Sea* in 1853. His legacy has been discredited because he joined the Confederate Navy in 1861.

[19] The first steam powered tugboat was launched in 1817. They were commonplace by the 1850s.

[20] The Sandy Hook Lighthouse, located inland from the tip of Sandy Hook, New Jersey is the oldest working lighthouse in the United States. It was designed and built on June 11, 1764.

[21] A sextant is a doubly reflecting navigation instrument that measures the angular distance between two visible objects. The primary use of a sextant is to measure the angle between an astronomical object and the horizon for the purposes of celestial navigation.

[22] The Second Opium War (1853 – 1858) was fought by Britain against China. The issues included the legalization of the opium trade, expansion of the transport of cheap laborers, opening all of China to British merchants and opium traffickers, and exempting foreign imports from internal transit duties.

[23] Diary of Eliza Gibson, August 12, 1855.

[24] The Agulhas Current is the western boundary current of the southwest Indian Ocean. It flows south along the east coast of Africa.

[25] To tack is to change the course of a sailing vessel by bringing the head into the wind and then causing it to fall off on the other side.

[26] An ensign is a flag, especially a naval one indicating nationality.

[27] A nautical mile is one sixtieth of a degree of latitude equal to about 6080 feet or 1853 meters.

[28] Spanish for the "Mouth of the Port of San Francisco."

[29] The quarterdeck is the stern area of a ship's upper deck.

[30] More properly called "Isla de Los Estados."

[31] The Drake Passage (also referred to as Mar de Hoces) is the body of water between South America's Cape Horn, Chile, and the South Shetland Islands of Antarctica. It is considered one of the most treacherous voyages for ships to make.

[32] A crow's nest is a structure in the upper part of the main mast of a ship or a structure that is used as a lookout point.

[33] A foretop is a platform around the head of the lower section of a sailing ship's foremast.

[34] Records show that a William Keller died in Talbottom, Georgia at age 74. Could possibly be him.

[35] A Free Mason is a member of an ancient fraternal organization called "The order of Free and Accepted Masons."

[36] The Panama Railroad, with New York financiers, completed the railroad in 1855. The first train departed on January 28, 1855.

[37] The Panama Canal did not exist at this time.

www.ingramcontent.com/pod-product-compliance
Ingram Content Group UK Ltd.
Pitfield, Milton Keynes, MK11 3LW, UK
UKHW020138250726
13967UKWH00002B/722

9 781471 077944